WHAT'S LURKING IN THIS HOUSE?

In This Kitchen

Nancy Harris

Raintree

Chicago, Illinois

www.heinemannraintree.com
Visit our website to find out
more information about
Heinemann-Raintree books.

To order:

☎ Phone 888-454-2279
💻 Visit www.heinemannraintree.com
to browse our catalog and order online.

2010 Raintree Library
an imprint of Capstone Global Library, LLC
Chicago, Illinois

Edited by Rebecca Rissman, Nancy Dickmann,
and Sian Smith
Designed by Joanna Hinton-Malivoire
Original illustrations © Capstone Global Library LLC, 2010
Illustrated by Kevin Rechin
Picture research by Tracy Cummins
Originated by Capstone Global Library Ltd
Printed and bound in China by Leo Paper
Products Ltd

14 13 12 11 10
10 9 8 7 6 5 4 3 2 1

**Library of Congress Cataloging-in-
Publication Data**
Harris, Nancy, 1956-
  In this kitchen / Nancy Harris.
    p. cm. -- (What's lurking in this house?)
  Includes bibliographical references and index.
  ISBN 978-1-4109-3725-4 (hc)
  ISBN 978-1-4109-3731-5 (pb)
1. Household pests--Juvenile literature. 2. Kitchens--Juve-
nile literature. 3. Hygiene--Juvenile literature. I. Title.
  TX325.H275 2010
  648'.7--dc22
                          2009022150

Acknowledgments
The author and publisher are grateful to the following for
permission to reproduce copyright material: Alamy p.**17**
(© Maximilian Weinzierl); Dwight Kuhn Photography p.**9**
(© Dwight Kuhn); Getty Images p.**12** (Jim Doberman);
Photo Researchers, Inc. pp.**7** (© Nigel Cattlin), **21** (©
Gusto), **23 bottom** (© Scimat), **25** (© Eye of Science),
27 bottom (© Cordelia Molloy); Photolibrary pp.**6**
(Imagesource), **28** (Digital Vision); Photoshot p.**11**
(Bruce Cocleman/Edward Snow); Shutterstock pp.**10**
(© PetrP), **13** (© Ronald van der Beek), **15 bottom** (©
Johanna Goodyear), **15 top** (© Studiotouch), **23 top**
(© Bochkarev Photography), **24** (© karovka), **27 top** (©
Gertjan Hooijer), **29 fly** (© Liew Weng Keong), **29 roach**
(© Connie Wade); Visuals Unlimited, Inc. pp.**19** (© Nigel
Cattlin), **20** (© Dr. James L. Castner).
Cover photograph of an American cockroach reproduced
with permission of FLPA (© Nigel Cattlin).

Some words are shown in bold, **like this**. You can find
out what they mean by looking in the glossary.

Contents

Is Something Lurking in This House?

A house is a place where you eat, sleep, work, and play. The kitchen is where food is kept. Have you ever thought about what might be living there with the food?

FUN FACT

You might think bathrooms are bad, but the kitchen can be the dirtiest room in the house!

Dinner Time!

You are helping to make dinner.
You go to a cupboard to get some
rice. What you find lurking there is
more than you expected!

Rice weevils are tiny creatures. You might find them living in rice, cereals, and other foods.

grain of rice

rice weevil

Who Is Eating Your Food?

Inside a cereal box you see mealworms munching away. You cannot miss them. They are golden brown. You look in the cupboard. Mealworms are also in the flour and macaroni.

mealworm

Some mealworms are almost one inch long! That's about the same length as a paper clip.

Mealworms are not worms. They are insects. As they grow up they change, or **metamorphose**, into beetles. They eat all day and at night.

FUN FACT

A mealworm can **shed**, or lose, its skin up to 20 times before becoming an adult.

skin

This black mealworm beetle is eating bread that has been left out.

Eating Mealworms

Birds and fish like to eat mealworms. So do some people. They say mealworms are very tasty. What do you think? Would a mealworm snack be a good idea?

FUN FACT

Mealworms are low in fat and can be a good source of food.

13

Feasting on Your Fruit!

Fruit flies are very small insects. You might see them swarming around your fruit bowl. They feast on fruit and vegetables that have been left out.

This shows a fruit fly up close.

actual size
of a fruit fly

Crawling Cockroaches

Another insect crawling in the kitchen could be a cockroach. They like to live in dark places, such as under a refrigerator. They also like warm and **moist**, or damp, places.

cockroach

In kitchens there are lots of dark places for cockroaches to hide.

Cockroaches have oval-shaped bodies. They have **antennae** and six legs. Some have wings. Cockroaches are hard to get rid of.

FUN FACT

Most cockroaches have at least 18 knees!

antennae

knees

wings

Cockroaches crawl around on your kitchen counters. They move around in your food and on your dishes. As they crawl, they may carry **germs** around your kitchen. Germs are very small living things that can make you sick.

cockroach

Putting lids on your bottles will help keep out cockroaches and germs!

ketchup

FUN FACT

Cockroaches can climb walls because they have little claws on their feet.

Watch Out for Germs!

Your kitchen is full of **germs**. Many germs are so small that you can only see them with a **microscope**. There are many types of germs.

Many germs can live in your kitchen sink.

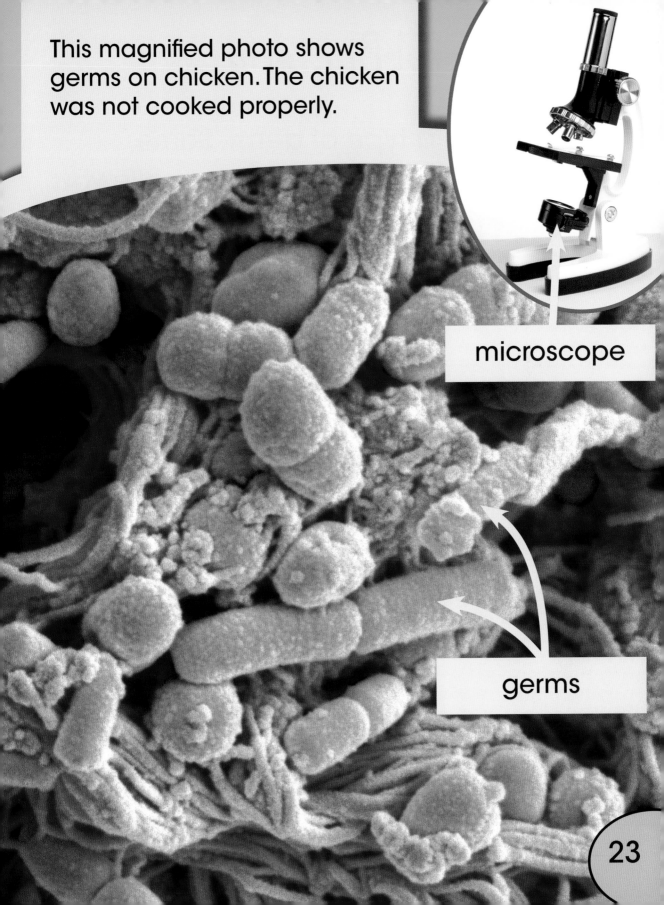

This magnified photo shows germs on chicken. The chicken was not cooked properly.

microscope

germs

Harmful Bacteria

Bacteria is a type of **germ**. Some bacteria in your kitchen can make you sick. Bacteria likes to eat dead pieces of plants and animals.

FUN FACT

Millions of bacteria can often be found on one kitchen sponge!

Kitchen sponge seen through a microscope.

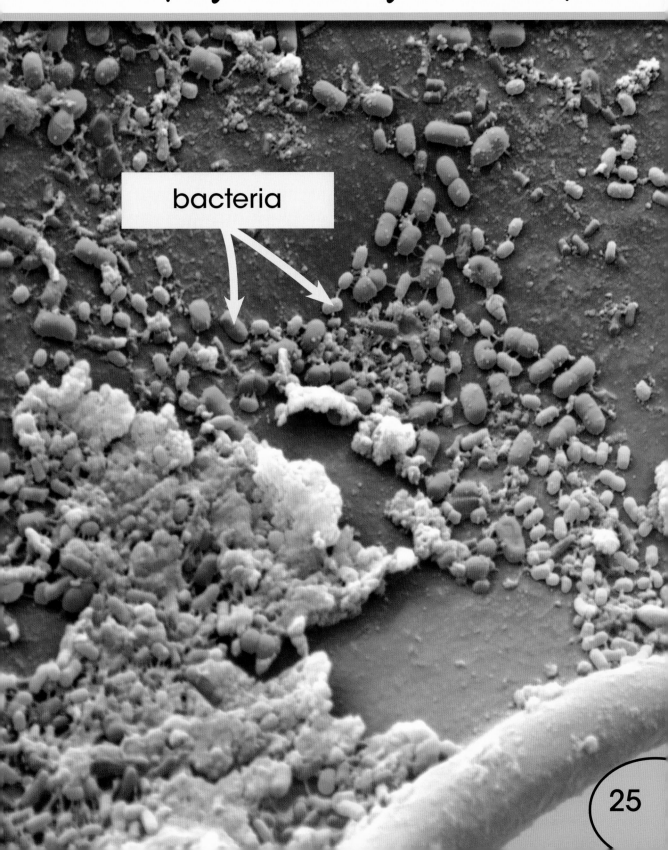

bacteria

Yuck! Mold

Mold is a small living thing. It can grow on food. Mold can grow on bread and cheese. It can be blue, white, or black. Look at food before you eat it. Mold can make you sick.

mold

mold

mold

Keeping It Clean

It is important to keep the kitchen clean. Putting dishes and sponges in a dishwasher can help kill **germs**. Counters can be washed with special soap. Cleaning up food scraps will help to keep away creatures. It will also help keep away **bacteria** and mold.

Fun Facts

Cockroaches can recognize each other by smell. Imagine if we could do that!

Cockroaches can swim. They can hold their breath for up to 40 minutes.

Cockroaches have white blood.

Mealworms will eat the bodies of dead mice or rats. They eat the bodies if they are old and dry.

Sadly for them, adult fruit flies only live for about 8 to 10 days.

Glossary

antennae a pair of feelers attached to the head of an insect

bacteria tiny living things. Bacteria are a type of germ.

germs tiny living things that can make you ill if they get inside your body

metamorphose to change into something else

microscope instrument used to see very small things such as germs

moist wet or damp

shed to take off and get rid of something

Find Out More

Books

Helget, Nicole. *Cockroaches.*
Mankato, MN: Creative Education, 2008.

Lindstrom, Karin. *Tiny Life on Plants.* Danbury, CT:
Children's Press, 2005.

Ridley, Sarah. *Where to Find Minibeasts:
Minibeasts in the Home.* Mankato, MN: Smart
Apple Media, 2009.

Rosenberg, Pam. *Yecch! Icky, Sticky, Gross Stuff in
Your House.* Mankato, MN: Child's World, 2008.

Slade, Suzanne. *What do You Know About Life
Cycles?* New York: PowerKids Press, 2008.

Websites

**http://www.songsforteaching.com/
jennyfixmanedutunes/germsgermsgerms.htm**
This Website has a song about germs and how
to stay healthy.

**http://www.pestworldforkids.org/
cockroaches.html**
This Website tells you about cockroaches
in general and describes four types of
cockroaches.

> **Find out**
>
> When do some cockroaches grow wings?

31

Index